D0916671

# OPEN LETTER FROM A TELEVISION VIEWER

# OPEN LETTER FROM A TELEVISION VIEWER

by

ROBERT MONTGOMERY

H
A HEINEMAN PAPERBACK

*Titles In This Series*

OPEN LETTER TO A YOUNG MAN (H10)
André Maurois

OPEN LETTER TO SALVADOR DALI (H11)
Salvador Dali

OPEN LETTER TO GOD (H12)
Robert Escarpit

OPEN LETTER TO A WOMAN OF TODAY (H13)
André Soubiran

OPEN LETTER AGAINST A VAST CONSPIRACY (H14)
Jules Romains

OPEN LETTER TO MEN (H15)
Françoise Parturier

OPEN LETTER TO NEWSPAPER READERS (H16)
John Tebbel

OPEN LETTER FROM A TELEVISION VIEWER (H17)
Robert Montgomery

OPEN LETTER TO MOSES AND MOHAMMED (H18)
Joel Carmichael

*Further books in this series are in preparation by American, British, French, German, Italian and Spanish authors.*

FIRST PRINTING 1968
Library of Congress Catalogue Card No. 68-9704

## A FOREWORD

The Open Letter series was conceived and developed as the platform for an international assembly of prominent people and established writers to discuss, dissect and delve into contemporary ideas and mores.

Each Open Letter is addressed to a segment of modern society, but its audience is all of us who do not accept the inevitable; who are seeking and questioning; and who are not afraid of being jolted out of complacence. Each letter is written with irony and charm; with optimism spiked with skepticism; and with humor laced with wit. Each letter is a personal polemic in which the author appeals to the mind rather than to the emotions; and chides with the épée rather than bludgeons with the hammer.

Books by American authors in this series are appearing in translation in Europe and Latin America. Publishers in other countries are adding their own titles to the series, which will appear in translation in the United States. Hence, a consortium of international writers will present, in companion Open Letters, divergent views, but always in keeping with the concept of the Open Letter series.

# OPEN LETTER FROM A TELEVISION VIEWER

# FOREWORD

This is an ill-tempered book, but not, I hope, one the reader will think merely polemic. The anger which inspires it is not an end in itself. It is intended to awaken in the television viewer some conception of the dangers inherent in the free-wheeling oligopoly which dominates the mass entertainment and information given to us nearly twenty-four hours a day by network television. I am especially angry and concerned about the threat this oligopoly holds for a free society.

In these pages the underlying theme is the difference between right and privilege. It is a difference the networks do not understand, or if they understand, choose to ignore. Broadcasting is *privileged* to use the air, which is owned by the American people. This privilege is derived from legislation enacted by the Congress of the United States, whose regulations are enforced by the governmental agency known as the

Federal Communications Commission. I contend that both privilege and responsibility have been evaded by the three great networks because they do not operate under government license, as individual stations must do. Consequently they behave as though they had a *right* to do whatever pleases them. This, I believe, is immoral and even illegal by any measurement.

I am angry and concerned, too, about the violence abroad in the land. It is well enough to say that we have always been a violent nation, from the days of the brawling frontier. But in nearly two hundred years of growth as a nation, is it unreasonable to expect that we should create something better than a society governed by the morals and the manners of the frontier? Instead, violence is so prevalent that our times are likely to be recorded in history as the Age of Violence. If it is, I believe that network television, a medium which has preached and conveyed violence on a mass basis unparalleled in history, must take a large share of the blame.

The networks have also contributed to the fabric of falsities which envelops our distressed society. Its lies about the nature of life and the human condition, the unreal world it creates, places a distorted mirror between man and his environment, until he is as neatly packaged as the programs and the commercials that make them possible.

Even more sinister, perhaps, is the cynicism engendered by the large corporations which control broadcasting. It is a cynicism about public taste, and it says quite clearly that these corporations believe people are basically too undiscriminating and of too low taste to want or deserve anything above the lowest common denominator, and that they will accept anything offered to them at that level. The Big Lie network broadcasting has created, and in which it appears to believe implicitly, is that the public doesn't want anything good in its television programing, and if it is given to them, will not accept it. The contempt of the network broadcasters for their public is scarcely concealed. They regard their viewers as little better than simple-minded fools. Possibly this could be the reason that in many American homes the TV set is usually referred to as the "idiot box."

It is important, I think, to draw a clear line between the medium and its use. As we were all informed and believed when television was new, it has the greatest potential for good of any communications instrument ever invented. Most of us still feel that this is true. At the same time, I think there are now millions of people who, like me, believe that television lost its way and fell among evil companions who have not only prevented it from realizing its potential but have turned it in another direction. Ironically, the technological advance of television has been spectacular. More than ever today it offers a brilliant promise. But sadly, there is no relationship between technology and the quality of what is being transmitted.

Another distinction must be made, one between the network entrepreneurs of television, and those who work for it in the lower echelons. The medium is full of extremely able and talented men, fully capable of realizing everything television is capable of doing. They do what they are permitted to do, and many of them are miserable doing it, praying for the day when, if ever, it will be possible to accomplish better things.

Nor would it be fair to assert that television does nothing worth commendation. Sometimes, by virtue of the sheer expertise of the people who work for it, television shows real flashes of the exciting medium it can be; in the live transmission of public events, it cannot be excelled. By and large, however, what is done well on television is done in spite of network control, not because of it.

These are the sources of ill temper in this book. The anger in its pages is the anger I have felt as one viewer who realizes he has no recourse, no way of protesting what the networks are doing to him. I write in the hope that one voice might became a great public chorus which shouts in a mighty thunder to the network moguls, "We are better than you think we are."

Television has been used successfully as a kind of baby sitter for animals in the zoo. While it plays on mindlessly, the animals are soothed by its flickering lights and noise level. Many Americans are beginning to feel like those animals, as though they were being used in the same way. And they are as helpless as the animals to get at their keepers —in this case, the networks. Some of those who are angry enough have gone back in large numbers to reading, as paperback sales and library circulations indicate. This is a salutary thing for the book trade, and one I would not discourage, but television has something to offer, too, if it can be released. No one now believes that television means the end of book reading, which has been previously threatened with extinction by bicycles, motion pictures, the automobile, and radio. In the right hands, telecasting could be the intelligent companion of books and reading.

I believe Americans are entitled to have their own television, and later in this book I shall present the case for public television, which is presently struggling to be born. Every American concerned about the quality of his life should do what he can to assist in that birth. For with it will come freedom from the restraints commercial television has placed upon us. Properly financed, public television will provide an atmosphere of freedom for those who conceive of the tube as something more than a money-making device, and a license to operate as more than a permit to get rich. To the citizen it will mean freedom to view what the commercial system, by its very nature, will not permit him to see.

This freedom is essential. Nothing less will do.

*The Television Viewer:*

At the outset, I offer you my sympathy. Certainly there can be no more frustrated body of people in the United States, where communications are concerned, than the millions who sit before their small screens night after night and watch the shifting patterns of inanity, whose intelligences quiver under a thousand insults, and have nowhere to turn to utter a complaint. Some few call up their local stations and get a polite, noncommittal answer if anyone cares to bother. Even fewer may think to write a letter to the Federal Communications Commission, and this will elicit a reassuring form reply but, in most cases, no action.

Not many direct their complaints to the source of their difficulty, the network which produced and transmitted the offending program. Yet this is where the damage originates, in that triopoly which determines what Americans shall see and hear on their television sets for the greater part of their viewing time. It is to this triopoly—the National Broadcasting Company, the Columbia Broadcasting System, and the American Broadcasting Company, the controllers of the tube—that I have addressed this open letter.

It is important that viewers understand the difference between their local stations and the network, and especially that they grasp the fundamental difference in the way each conducts its business. The local station is licensed by the Federal Communications Commission, and it is subject to a body of laws laid down by the FCC, through the authority of Congress. The Commission has a final power over the local station because it has the authority to decide on whether an individual broadcaster's license shall be renewed.

The network, on the other hand, is not subject to regulation. It is a private business enterprise which is not under any form of control except the tax laws. The three networks control absolutely what is seen on television, except for the small percentage of programing originating in the local stations. Their standards govern what is seen, and business is their business.

No other form of communication is quite like broadcasting, and that is why the position of the networks is unique. Newspapers are private property and so are magazines, but the air which transmits radio and television belongs to all the people. That is why Congress undertook to control what is broadcast over it, licensing first radio stations, then television, and creating the FCC, with its regulatory powers over individual stations. The networks are a business creation, superimposed on the basic structure of broadcasting. Thus what was meant originally to be a privilege—ownership of a station—has somehow been converted by the network owners into something they quite obviously consider a right. When their conduct of the networks is attacked, they retreat under the flag of private enterprise. They also plead that they are merely giving the public what it wants, offering the rating system as proof. As we shall see, in another section of this letter, here is an argument of formidable cynicism which not even those who make it really believe.

What has been lost, or nearly lost, in the situation created by network broadcasting is a precious freedom, not only on the part of the viewer, who is subject to the dictation of the networks, but also on the part of those who are or ought to be involved in the creation of programs—the skilled artists, technicians, managers, and leaders who are either stifled by the present system or who have had to turn their talents to some other medium. People with talent and ideas have a hard time with the triopoly. Some of them leave in a cloud of public awareness. Many others simply resign and go elsewhere.

Freedom and excellence: these are the criteria by which television broadcasting ought to be judged. People can work and grow in it creatively only if these conditions prevail, and if they believe that television is the medium through which they can express themselves best.

This idea is the essence of the recent Carnegie Commission Report on Educational Television. "... What we recommend is freedom," the report declares, with more passion than is usually found in a sober investigative body of fifteen people. "We seek freedom from the constraints, however necessary in their context, of commercial television. We seek for educational television freedom from the pressures of inadequate funds. We seek for the artist, the technician, the journalist, the scholar, and the public servant freedom to create, freedom to innovate, freedom to be heard in this most far-reaching medium. We seek for the citizen freedom to view, to see programs that the present system, by its incompleteness, denies him . . ."

Reading this, the viewer may well ask himself, "If this is such a splendid thing for educational television, why isn't it possible for commercial television too? Are the proprietors of commercial television *against* freedom? Do they discourage freedom to create and innovate, and freedom to be heard? Are the artist, the technician, the journalist, the scholar, and the public servant to be denied these freedoms on the air which belongs to us?"

What, he may well conclude, is going on here? Obviously, his own freedom is being abridged, as the Report implies when it seeks for him the "freedom to view." Until now, he may have imagined he *had* that freedom, but now it appears that the only way he can expect to get it is through educational television. (Public television, as proposed by the recently passed Public Television Act, would be programing in the general interest, without commercials, financed by public money —that is, tax dollars. Educational television, as presently constituted, does both teaching broadcasts and cultural programming, but is financed by foundations, private donations, and in some cases by school systems as well.)

I assume that you, the viewer, are not against either educational or public television, that you wish them both well in their fight to be seen and for stature. It is no denigration of educational television, however, to say that it is not designed for the mass audience, nor should it be. (No one knows what shape public television will take.) Yet this simple fact should never be construed to mean that the viewer in that mass audience must sit and absorb whatever the networks choose to feed his mass mind, on the assumption that he does not deserve anything better, and wouldn't look at it if he had it.

It is difficult, I grant, for the viewer to identify his enemy. All he sees on the screen is the omniscient eye, the spreading peacock, and the familiar logotype which identify the networks. He reads their self-congratulatory advertising in his newspaper and gets the impression from it that he is a fortunate man indeed to possess a television set capable of bringing him such wonders, such selfless devotion to his needs. To the viewer, the network is a faceless entity—faceless except for the logotype—and he is not conscious of what mighty forces it controls.

If he were a stockholder, he would understand better when he reads the annual report. I have before me one such report. It tells the shareholders of the Columbia Broadcasting System, Inc., what their company owned at the end of 1967, and how much it had earned. This colossus stands on four legs. One is the broadcast group, including the news division, the television network division, the television stations division, the CBS radio division, and the CBS films division. The Columbia group includes Columbia records, the direct-marketing services division, the international division, and the musical instruments division. Its "Holt group" consists of Holt, Rinehart & Winston, the book publishing company; Creative Playthings, Inc.; the CBS Learning Center; and Bailey Films and Film Associates. The fourth leg, or Comtec Group, lists the laboratories division, the television services division, and the CBS-EVR division. At the tail of the colossus, moving scarcely enough to be called wagging, are the New York Yankees.

In terms of dollars, CBS earned $904 million in net sales during 1967. Its net income was $53 million. The National Broadcasting Company earned $488,810,000 in 1965, and the American Broadcasting Company recorded $361,631,000 in the same year. Total industry revenue in 1967 from time sales was nearly $2 billion, and television's total worth in time and talent was $200 million over and above $2 billion.

These are the dimensions of the huge forces behind the eye, the peacock, and the logotype. They made so much money by transmitting to a hundred million television screens a hodgepodge of situation comedy, westerns, sports, and, as the viewer of 1968 ought to remind himself, more violence than ever. Riots and war were added in larger measure to the already overflowing bucket of bloody crime and western shows.

No country can begin to match (nor would it care to) the flood of violence which pours from our television screens. Homicide and sadism, cruelty of every variety, are the stock in trade of what passes for entertainment. This is not to say that violence doesn't saturate every other medium as well, but where one can selectively read a newspaper, magazine, or book, television is like the motion pictures in demanding exclusive attention to what is on the screen. In the few American cities which have several channels, there is some choice, but for most people, if they are going to watch television at all, it is predominant violence or nothing. If this period of American life goes down in history as the Age of Violence, television must accept some of the responsibility.

It is sometimes argued that the depiction of violence has no influence on the viewer, but it is becoming increasingly clear that a numbness, even an indifference, to sudden death is becoming a frightening characteristic of American life, as though dying were no longer any more than an incident as casual as it is on the small screen, where it may be followed in five seconds by a toothpaste commercial. When the citizen turns away from real violence with his now familiar plea, "I don't want to get involved," he expresses his feeling of non-involvement as he watches safely before his screen the torturing and killing of other human beings. There he is not involved, and he is not moved to be involved by the cry for help in the streets either. So intense has his fantasy life become that he may even expect that cry to end in another commercial.

The ratings tell us that a vast number of people are watching television—how many in reality, and how many in relation to any single program we don't know in truth, but in any case enough to convince us that we are, in greater or less degree, addicts. In the numbers game, however, with its shifting claims and ruthless dictation of what will survive and what will perish, a most important element has been omitted. Ratings do not, and cannot, tell us the reaction of the viewer to what he sees.

Because a show commands a high rating does that mean twenty-five million people are watching it with absorbed fascination, or are they looking out of habit or boredom? There is strong empirical evidence to indicate that people talk a lot while they watch television as they do at the zoo, and this habit has caused a disturbing change in motion-picture audiences, whose conversation often competes with the dialogue on the large screen. But there is still a great deal we don't know about viewer reaction. The ratings give us only numbers, and since there is no one the viewer can get in touch with to tell how he feels, except in isolated instances, it is impossible to tell whether he is really, as the broadcasters insist, getting what he wants. There is, after all, no obligation on the part of the public to demand better television. The responsibility is in the hands of the broadcasters who are using the public air.

Network broadcasters should be reminded that it is not hard to attract large numbers of people. You can attract a crowd with a hanging.

As viewers, it is time to ask ourselves again what the function of television is, and what we are entitled to expect from it—from the privilege we have granted to the broadcasters to use the air. If we go to the bedrock of American democracy, the answer becomes plain. As the historian George Bancroft put it, our country was "designed to organize social union through the establishment of personal freedom," and after our country was organized, "thought obtained for itself free utterance . . . (and) industry was commissioned to follow the bent of its own genius."

These principles are implicit in free broadcasting, as the House Committee on Interstate and Foreign Commerce noted in its 1963 report on television, in which it described the "genius" of competitive American industry, in the interest of the public, as "commissioned" to "build bridges" over which might pass "the ideas and cultural aspirations of our free, pluralistic society."

This is the splendid theory on which broadcasting is based. The assumption is that the interests of broadcasters and advertisers, and indeed everyone who uses the publicly owned channels of broadcasting, are not in conflict with the high public purposes which underlie our society. "It further assumes," said the Committee, "that communication of ideas and cultural aspirations essential to the development and progress of our society will not be unduly impeded by commercial convenience or selfish interest or Government edict."

Obviously, this happy union of interests has not occurred. At a time when, as never before, it is essential to employ all the intellectual and spiritual resources we possess, the broadcasters have failed to play the part that President Eisenhower so well defined for them in 1956 when he called them "crusaders" in democracy's cause, a "mighty force in our civilization" capable of furthering our national effort to "understand ourselves" and "promote the truth about our country abroad," thereby helping us to "earn our way to peace."

We have certainly deviated a long way from that ideal—so far that there is some reason to wonder if we can ever make our difficult way back. The broadcasters' contention that it is not wrong "to appeal to most of the people most of the time," true as that may be in theory, has actually resulted in the principles of marketing efficiency being applied to the appeal of programing, rather than the paramount public interest. It would be difficult to find many of the products of the "spiritual, cultural, and intellectual forces at work in our mobile society," as the Committee puts it, in the day-to-day programing of the networks.

What is the missing ingredient here? Where is the fast-acting powder that will give us quick, quick relief from our ills? It is the absence of any effort on the part of the broadcasters to study the impact of television on the people who watch it, except in commercial terms. There is not one individual in the entire broadcasting industry who is presently addressing himself to that study. We have no realistic idea of what is happening to the viewers of our country who spend hour after hour sitting in front of their television screens, absorbing or not absorbing the most incredible salmagundi ever offered to a people.

Not only is the programing content based on a spurious reality, but the advertising which finances it, running into many millions of dollars, is essentially "a bill for falsehood," as William Ernest Hocking points out in his *Strength of Men and Nations*. For it is not that advertising "lies in regard to facts—this it hesitates to do," Hocking notes; "its falsities are *lies of emotion*. . . . In any civilization *falsehoods of feeling are more deadly than falsehoods of fact.* They are also more insidious; for they are irrefutable—they do not argue, they infect the mind . . ."

The conviction grows that the viewer is as numb to everything else as he is to violence, that he is being progressively brainwashed until he responds to practiced commercial stimuli with all the enthusiasm of a laboratory animal.

I have addressed myself to the triopoly of broadcasting in this Open Letter, but here I speak to the viewer himself, and I must say to him that he *need* not be brainwashed, he *need* not submit to being given what he is constantly told he likes. Moreover, he has a basic right to demand something else, and if that demand is unlikely, then the broadcasting industry must be called to account, to consider the responsibility which it assumed when it was granted license to use the public air in the interest of its public owners.

There are ways by which viewers can make themselves heard. It may be argued that they are ineffective ways, but they need not be if the protest is numerically strong enough. If the networks are so sensitive to ratings, is there any reason to suppose they would be any less responsive to viewer opinion, if it were on anything like the same scale?

If you are disturbed by what you see, write a letter of protest to the sponsor of the show and another to the network which broadcast it. The former may earn you a public relations form letter in reply; the latter will probably be ignored. Sponsors, however, react to viewers' letters, and if there were enough of them on any given subject, they would react strongly.

Send carbon copies of your letters to the Federal Communications Commission and to your congressmen. It will be a measure of your concern if you take the trouble to find out who your congressmen are, and where to reach the FCC. These letters in themselves may not bring any more encouraging response at first than those sent to sponsors or networks, but if enough of them reach government, government will respond, as we have seen in other instances of national public indignation. But the indignation needs to be demonstrably widespread, otherwise the complaints may be dismissed as the isolated outrages of the minority who are always disaffected by something in public life.

I believe there is more than enough dissatisfaction with commercial television in America to make an impression. It only needs to be expressed.

*The Family:*

In the early days of television, the tube was widely regarded as a medium which might reunite the disintegrating American family, on the premise, no doubt, that the family that watches together stays together. Subsequent events have proved this to be a sociological error, for reasons not altogether within television's control. But if it has failed to unite, it has at least succeeded in getting the attention of every family member, for differing reasons and with a different response from each one.

If the family does not often watch as a group, it isn't only because tastes are different, but because the point of view of television programing is, in reality, *against* the family unit rather than for it. From the manufacturers' standpoint, the natural difference in taste is an excellent thing, since it leads to two-set and three-set households. At the beginning, juvenile domination of the family set was so complete that it became a stock joke in the comic's repertory; but as creeping affluence has set in, more and more families have simply sequestered the children with their own set, out of sight and sound. The family shows that once dominated television programing are disappearing, or at least are taking a less prominent role. Now the tremendous expansion of sports on television has given the male audience so much to look at, especially football, that even *The New York Times* has taken editorial note of the hapless weekend television football widows who lose their husbands to the tube from early September to the middle of January.

As for the women, they are given the ghetto of daytime television game shows and soap opera. At night, everybody goes to the movies on the small screen, but the children may be watching one and their parents another, in places where there is enough choice of stations.

As we look in on our little American family, distributed around the house before the glowing screens, or clustered before a single tube in homes where economy has enforced togetherness, we can be fairly certain that there are few, if any, families that are entirely happy with what they see. There has been some statistical evidence to show that the size of the television audience is actually declining; its attention span may have declined even more.

Whatever their numbers or their absorption may be in any given instance, it can be said that the shows they watch have a common denominator: fantasy. As Hollywood once created an unreal world, which at least some Americans could distinguish from the real thing (although many foreigners cannot to this day), so television has built its own series of fantasies. Some of them are innocent enough, depending on devices which are frankly theatrical, and in which no one is expected truly to believe. They are contemporary fairy tales, written for grown-up children—pleasant illusions of a kind which people must have in some measure to survive.

The trouble is that the most successful of these shows immediately lead to a proliferation of similar programs, because television follows Hollywood in its urge to imitate successful patterns until the last dollar can be wrung from an idea. Thus there is a multiplication of fantasy, where a little less would have been more than enough, and there are periods of saturation in which one kind of show is repeated endlessly in a dozen different formats.

But let us make some effort to examine how television programs affect the consciousness of the family members, and how the networks, in their competitive zeal to exploit every possible interest, are pushing fantasy to the outer limits of acceptability.

Father, the head of the house, is by this time accustomed to seeing himself portrayed in the situation comedies as an amiable, bewildered idiot who is skillfully manipulated by the other members of the household to get what they want. He accepts this portrayal, perhaps, because there is just enough truth in it to make Father feel that he would be betraying reality as well as destroying the stereotype if he protested. In some respects, our matriarchal society has done its work well.

Yet Father more or less cheerfully suffers the clichés of the situation shows in the knowledge that on Saturdays and Sundays, and during the week in the case of baseball, he can reinforce his ego and find an outlet for his carefully suppressed aggressions in televised sports. In their anxiety to take advantage of this widespread male preoccupation, the networks have found that it is not enough to cover the standard sports —baseball, football, and basketball—but others, like hockey, soccer, bowling, billiards, hunting, fishing, tennis, wrestling, and amateur skiing must be added. And even this is not enough. Esoteric events like demolition derbies, in which old cars are driven around tracks and into obvious collisions with the threat of death in the background, like mechanized bullfights, are labeled sport. Anything a man does when he is not in the office appears to be considered a legitimate sport today, and one can be certain that someone, somewhere has organized it to the point where it can be shown on television for money.

Professional sports have captured the market, but there is amateur football (if the college sport can be called that), and amateur tennis (what remains of it), and other amateur endeavors which television is not above making a profit out of while the players, in most cases, get nothing. "Amateur" in sports broadcasting is a little like "public domain" in publishing—that is, production may cost something, but the producer gets the basic product for nothing.

Sports are literal, in spite of the mystique built up around them individually, yet fantasy enters heavily into their telecasting. There is a sharp contrast between the technical excellence of sports coverage, where one can only admire the deft and imaginative uses of the camera, and the fantasy life of the sportscaster. He lives in the best of all possible worlds. Nothing in the least critical is ever said about a player or a team, unless it is hedged around with so many qualifications that it becomes meaningless. A cheery optimism prevails. When a football player lies on the turf, obviously in agony, the announcer remarks with buoyant assurance, "Joe seems to be shaken up a little bit down there, but he'll be all right." A free-for-all breaks out on the field, and the announcer remarks gaily, "Seems to be a little high spirits among the boys, but it doesn't mean anything." Or again, referring to a small riot in the stands, "Some of the fans seem to be protesting that decision, folks, but the police have matters well in hand." Meanwhile, presumably upon the advice of counsel, the camera resolutely focuses on the goal posts, the vista beyond the stadium, the scoreboard, a passing airplane, the Goodyear blimp—anything but where the action is taking place.

The women fare little better in the hours of the day set aside for their particular enchantment. The daytime game shows, suffused with false geniality, are based quite simply on human greed. There is not much of the Olympic spirit visible in the race to win huge piles of merchandise or substantial bundles of money. Their worst offense is the false system of values they encourage.

Drama, derived from old-fashioned radio soap opera, has not changed substantially from the days when it could only be heard, and Helen Trent was everyone's heroine. That is, the principal ingredients are still there—the operations, the divorces, the tangled love affairs, the weepy situations. But something else has been added, and television demonstrates that it has changed with the prevailing climate of manners and morals. *Peyton Place*, and its spectacular success in every medium, has laid its fevered hands on Helen Trent's descendants. Many contemporary soap operas are based on the idea that inside every small community is a cesspool trying to get out, and television affords it an opportunity to emerge.

While it would be fatuous to argue that life in American towns is a tender reminiscence of *David Harum*, at the same time *Peyton Place* and its many imitative offspring are hardly typical of the way life is lived between the Appalachians and the Rockies. How the people who do live in those towns feel about the way their villages and small cities are depicted is apparent to anyone who makes speaking tours. Nothing stirs up a more violent response—not even Vietnam—than a discussion of the *Peyton Place* influence, especially in the soap operas. "Livid" is the only way to describe the women on this subject.

If sports are upbeat, it may be added, television drama, particularly in the daytime, is downbeat, If a program makes the mistake of holding out any hope for its victims of concentrated misfortune, it becomes a candidate for oblivion and often goes off the air in rather short order. Because women are exposed to this kind of thing so much more than the men, it is not surprising that these conflicting moods of sports optimism and soap opera pessimism are often in collision on the domestic front, although not in such bald terms. The broadcaster may pooh-pooh the idea, but it would be hard to argue that television is a reducer of tension in the home.

When sports and drama are over for the day, viewers are treated to one of the most depressing examples of television's inability to think for itself. The idea of the "late show," of the live or semi-live variety, originated with the now historic Jack Paar program. Whatever one may have thought of Paar—and the controversy lingers on—no one doubts that he established a lively format of late-night entertainment, and by the sheer force of his perverse, unusual personality, millions of Americans were kept up long past their bedtime. The parade of "guests" was secondary to Paar's own offbeat, unpredictable humor—a refreshing change from the dreary sameness of most television comedy, although counterbalanced by his overbearing graciousness to public figures.

But then Paar retired, leaving behind him the vacuum the broadcasters most abhor —a large segment of time otherwise relatively unprofitable unless occupied by an entertainer with a huge and devoted audience. Apparently it did not occur to anyone that something else might be done with the time, something as fresh and original as Paar himself had contributed. The drive was on at once to find another "personality" to replace Paar, one who might possibly hold the Paar audience to that channel. At the same time, the other networks made efforts, as they had for some time, to find suitable competition.

As everyone knows, Johnny Carson succeeded Jack Paar—same basic format, same offbeat humor, same kind of appeal to the same audience. Not surprisingly, in this case, the same success story was repeated. One of the competing networks developed its own late-night show as competition, using the comedian Joey Bishop as Carson's counterpart. Needless to say, except for the style and personality of the two entertainers, the shows were not noticeably different from each other, and their formats were no more than a city block removed from Paar's. It was observed, too, that Mr. Bishop did not elicit from his audience the joyous response he got from his cast, whose laughter was a depressing mixture of professional conditioned reflex and professional fear.

Those whose attention might wander during these plotless late-evening revels are invited to abandon personalities and look at old movies. The vintages stretch backward as the hours slip forward toward dawn. In the latest night hours, the tube is heavy with nostalgia for the earliest days of the talkies. Is this because the networks think older people stay up half the night? They know better. The more expensive movies, made at a much more recent date, and capable of attracting far more sponsor money, come first, beginning as early as nine or nine-thirty. Age begins to set in after midnight as revenues decline.

The popularity of old movies (and new ones, for that matter) on television is an astonishing fact of life. More and more, the broadcasters are filling the hours with celluloid, overjoyed by this trend of events, since nothing is cheaper to produce, and with a clutch of commercials coming in at ten-minute intervals, nothing is more profitable, on a cost basis. It is a most damning indictment of television programing, however, to remember that movies made twenty years or more ago are considered by the viewers as better than anything produced today. So popular and profitable are these pictures that television is becoming virtually a continuous showing of motion pictures, from early morning to the last hours before dawn —almost around the clock. Nearly thirty years of commercial television, and the best we can do is a facsimile of the grind houses on Forty-second Street!

Commercials, of course, are more annoying if there is a movie worth watching than they are in the ordinary course of programing, where the commercial break is so often the signal for conversation, refreshment, or a momentary retreat into some other occupation. Motion pictures demand a kind of concentration not present in the other media, and while the commercial breaks so close together are hard enough to bear in themselves, what they do to a sense of what the director was trying to convey, if anything, is lost—as some of the directors themselves have been saying in trying to preserve their work from mutilation.

It seems an exercise in futility at this late date to say over again, wearily, what so many of us know about commercials—that they are too loud, too frequent, unbelievable, and unutterably tiresome. We are familiar, too, with the argument of the broadcasters, which comes down to the truism that it is the sponsors' money which makes programs possible under our free system of private enterprise, so that any kind of insult to the ears or intelligence must be borne because to protest is, by implication, to be against the American way of life, and to be asking for that bête noire, public television.

It is also said, frequently, that not all commercials are dreadful, that wit and skill are being exercised more frequently than before, and this is true. But it is also true that in a long day's viewing, these splendid examples of wit and skill are so rare that they stand out in bold relief against the wasteland.

What would happen to commercials, one wonders, if the words "new" and "improved" were suddenly declared obscene and unfit for transmission? The poverty of imagination, of ideas, would be disclosed in only one of its many shocking aspects.

Hocking has something to tell us about this, too. As consumers of goods, he points out, "We are constant practitioners of value-judgments, and as constantly in need of teaching." And he goes on: "One aspect of our major educational lapse lies in this perhaps unexpected quarter. We have a rising standard of living—the highest in the world, some say. As a companion piece to the rising standard—rising in terms of multiform easings, cushionings, amusings, and toolings for our various original and multiplying desires—we have also a rising *cost* of living. This cost is greatly swollen by a newly inflated factor, that of advertising, a presumably necessary expenditure if ever-changing goods are to be made known to potential users. (A market of staples needs no advertising; we always know where potatoes are to be had: it is the 'improved model' that requires public education.) Advertising is now magnified in importance in order to present the multiplying novelties to *the entire market area;* but, mind you, to present them in such a light that each competing novelty can be made to appear *superior to every other!*

". . . I do not here speak of the resulting clamor for our limited fund of attention. The right to invade our peace through conventional channels is part of our national liberty, including the sacred right of a free speech and press to mislead the misleadable and to distract the already distraught. I do not speak of this ubiquitous intrusion, pressing to destroy even the peace of the rural neighborhood and the beauty of an unspoiled nature. I speak only of the radical and unalienable interest in *truth*."

The response of women to television is a powerful one. It can be fairly said that they no longer see themselves in the mirror; they view themselves reflected in the tube—in that fantasy tube where all women are beautiful and seductive and equally efficient in kitchen and bedroom by virtue of the products which paint their image on the screen. Here are Hocking's "practitioners of value-judgments," with a vengeance.

And so, in the family group, we come at last to the child. For a long time he came first, it is true, but with his own set and his own thoughts he can be safely entrusted to sit in his room and watch without disturbing anything—except possibly the world of tomorrow.

The question remains, is he disturbing himself? It is true that violence makes children insensitive, and that constant viewing induces a kind of hypnosis in which order, more productive activity, is suspended for hours at a time. The indictment, however, is larger.

An American child in his formative years, subjected to constant infusions of television programing, can hardly avoid growing up with the idea that the only way to settle any really serious discussion is to kill the man who disagrees with you, and since the child has no identification with the death he sees on the screen, it becomes as impersonal and meaningless as the images themselves.

He is also subjected to a distortion of history. Because of the pervasive censorship which extends through all the media, from textbooks to the tube, preventing the depiction of history in any form except clichés guaranteed not to offend any pressure group, the child sees only fantasy history. There is, indeed, a general distortion of reality always present on the tube—a "good guys and bad guys" point of view which removes all troubling complexities from the viewer's mind. This is coupled with a smoothing blandness designed to prevent even "goodness" and "badness" from appearing too extreme, so that no one, especially the viewer, will be disturbed.

What, one might ask, can be expected from a generation exposed from earliest childhood to this kind of pap? Ignorance, certainly, and it is in abundant supply in our society. Some observers of that society argue that world civilization is in danger of annihilation not so much from the hydrogen bomb as from human greed and stupidity, both qualities which television carefully cultivates for profit.

The family responds to these appeals directed toward the worst qualities of its membership simply because the sugarcoating is so smooth that the pills have been swallowed in lethal quality before it is apparent what their ultimate effect may be.

This is not to say that nothing worthwhile ever appears on the tube for family viewing. Television shows us from time to time what it can do in the way of education, of cultural enlightenment, of broadening the frontiers of the mind, of showing us that the world is full of wonders and delights as well as trivialities and futilities and horrors. But the urge to make the dollar in the easiest possible way, following the lines of easiest mass acceptance, is irresistible to the broadcasters whose minds have never reached beyond the stockholders to the area of public responsibility.

Against this kind of indifference, the American family still has no protection.

*The Politicians:*

In addressing the politicians, I must speak more in the first person. That comes naturally, because I have had the privilege of serving in the White House and under two Presidents—Franklin D. Roosevelt and Dwight D. Eisenhower. Their tenures encompassed the use of the media in the Presidency. I watched Mr. Roosevelt giving his celebrated Fireside Chats, those broadcasts which disclosed for the first time what radio could do for politics by putting a President in immediate touch with the whole nation at the same time. Then, as General Eisenhower's special consultant on television, I saw the influence of broadcasting stretched to a horizon not yet clearly defined, through the awesome potential of the tube.

This power frightens some people, and certainly in the hands of a successful demagogue it takes no extraordinary imagination to foresee that television could be the strong right arm of a dictatorship, as indeed it has already become in some parts of the world. But I believe the tube could also be a force for good, capable not only of improving politics as a calling but of raising the quality of the political servant—if it is not overused.

So new, relatively, is the use of television as a political weapon that it is not clearly understood, even by those who employ it. Some politicians do not comprehend (nor do most viewers) the distinction between a performance and an appearance. What is quite clearly realized, however, is television's function as a kind of mass lie detector, which paradoxically can be a potent mass persuader in the hands of those who know how to use it. The deadly clarity of the camera's vision strips away pretense as though it were tissue paper, revealing with the merciless bluntness of a scalpel the underlying personality characteristics which radio can conceal, and which may even be lost in the sweaty excitement of real-life confrontation in a large auditorium.

We have seen the terrible power of television at work, most notably in the debates between John F. Kennedy and Richard M. Nixon as rival candidates. (I shall give my own view of that battle presently.) Often the disaster occurs before our eyes, in a single, swift exposure, as when a former governor of a New England state arrived to make a speech at a national convention, and before the horrified gaze of his staff, exposed himself to millions as a mealy-mouthed spellbinder of the old school whom no one would have believed for a minute at such close range. It was the end of his political career, and rightly so.

I became aware of television's political power while I was learning of its myth-making abilities. So enchanted are people by what they think the medium is able to do that they seem to regard those who work with it as some kind of latter-day Merlins. While I was in Washington, a legend grew up about what I was doing in the White House, and a curious set of stories emanated from the capital, declaring or implying, depending on the source, that I was doing everything for Mr. Eisenhower from making him up for television appearances to instructing him in how to give a theatrical performance when he came before the cameras.

None of these stories was true. I am not a makeup man, and as for trying to show the General how to give a performance, what an impertinence it would have been for me to have tried to influence a President with Mr. Eisenhower's broad background of experience, and tell him how to deal with people. He was quite capable of that without my advice.

What I did attempt to do was, in a sense, to educate him about the uses of television, a medium unfamiliar to him except as a casual viewer when he entered the White House. People had told him a good many horror stories about what he could or could not do with television, and most of them were untrue. "What have they been telling you?" I asked him. Well, for example, he said, he had been told he would have to sit quietly behind a desk and not move about, or it would be distracting to the audience. No truth in that, I assured him. He believed, too, that there were some things he could say on television, and some he couldn't. Nonsense, I assured him. It was his duty to say whatever he wanted to say, and it was my duty to see to it that no technical nonsense or jargon would interfere with that duty.

Since the President brought the staff-and-line procedure of his military days to the White House with him, I had numerous conferences with his aides, rather than with him, on whether television should be employed in specific instances. Whatever was decided at that level would be presented to him for final decision. Nearly always, he accepted our advice.

One of the first of these conferences had to do with whether the President's press conferences ought to be televised. I thought they should be; others did not. The issue was decided by examing the transcripts of previous press conferences and the subsequent use made of them by the media. We wanted to see if there was any difference in those covered both by the press and television, and those by television alone. We found that the quality of the coverage was better when all the media were represented. Apparently reporters made a greater effort to be accurate when the cameras were making a visual record which could be examined later to prove the truth or falsity of a written impression.

The television education of the President began as soon as I got to the White House, and for an hour and a half listened to his remembrances of what he had been told by a great variety of people in and out of the medium, including Winston Churchill. He accepted my advice without reservation. As far as television was concerned, no authority was to supersede mine.

There was one moment during my tenure at the White House, however, when the President's faith in me was severely tested. It occurred soon after Mr. Eisenhower suffered his first illness, his now famous heart attack. Secretary of State John Foster Dulles had just returned from an important conference in Europe, and had given a private report to the President on what he had learned there. Mr. Eisenhower was so impressed by what his Secretary of State had told him that he wanted Dulles to go on television and repeat his report for the benefit of the whole nation.

Since the Secretary was not noted for his inspirational effect on audiences, we agreed on a format for his presentation which would be more informal and something of a novelty for a Presidential broadcast. It was to be a question-and-answer program, in which Mr. Eisenhower himself would be the questioner and Dulles would provide the answers (or the substance of them) he had given the President in private conversation. This was not, to be sure, a new idea. It is well known that an audience can be persuaded to listen to a man by the device of having another man on stage or camera listening to him.

Another important element involved in this broadcast was the question of the President's health. He was still recovering from his illness, and the unfounded rumor had spread that he was incapable of appearing in public and that this was why Secretary Dulles had been chosen to make the public report that otherwise might have been expected from the President himself. My problem was to prevent Mr. Eisenhower from being kept off screen while Dulles was speaking because it would dispose of the rumors if he could be shown listening as well as asking questions, and in good health (as in fact he was) during the program.

There was a conference in the Cabinet room at which I explained carefully both to the President and the Secretary that I was going to show both of them on the screen, and that Mr. Eisenhower was to give the appearance of listening to the Secretary's answers to his questions, not only because it was ordinary good manners but to aid Dulles in making the impression everyone wanted him to make. That would require a bit of acting on the President's part, since he knew by heart everything the Secretary was going to say.

Both men agreed to the plan, and in time we went to the President's office for the broadcast. I could not, of course, dictate the format of the show to the producer who represented the network pool for the broadcast; I could only ask him if he would consider putting both men on the screen. Fortunately, the director understood at once what I wanted to do and why, and said he thought it was an excellent idea.

The program began to unfold, but to our chagrin and horror, it did not turn out at all the way we had planned. The President asked the questions well enough—then sat back while Dulles answered; however, the President appeared to pay little if any attention to the answers. He acted exactly as I'm sure he felt, as though he had heard it all before. On the screen he seemed profoundly bored. It was quickly obvious that the audience was soon going to be even more disinterested than he was, but they had the option of switching off. I did what little could be done, getting word to the director as the broadcast went on and asking him to use separate shots instead, cutting from one man to the other, with the emphasis on Dulles, but by that time it was too late. The damage had been done.

To this day, I'm not sure what happened. Either the President was so preoccupied that he did not really hear what was said in the Cabinet room conference, or else he heard but, in the pressure of being on the air, simply forgot. In either case, he was totally unconscious of the effect he was creating, which became plain when we ran the tape of the show after the broadcast. The President was much upset. Unwittingly, he could see, he had done Secretary Dulles a real disservice.

Mr. Eisenhower might well have blamed me for this particular disaster. Characteristically, however, he only remarked when the tape had run out, turning to me: "I'm sure you must be as unhappy about this as I am." That was a profound understatement. Yet I could not remind him that I had warned him to appear interested in the Secretary's answers, even though he knew them so well. One does not reprimand the President for errors of omission—or anything else, for that matter.

Politicians have been learning the uses of television rapidly since then. Mr. Eisenhower himself learned much before he retired from office. Yet even so astute a campaigner as Nixon had not learned enough in 1960 to avoid a fundamental mistake. It was not the mistake many people suppose. We have all heard about the failure of the makeup man to remove the Nixon five o'clock shadow, and there are those who still believe that this was part of a Kennedy plot. In other versions, the camera operator gets the blame (whether or not in the pay of the Kennedys) for taking better shots of Mr. Kennedy than of Nixon. People who embrace any theory of conspiracy wholeheartedly are certain both the makeup man and the cameraman were involved in the plot.

There was, needless to say, no conspiracy. The makeup man did his job as well as possible, and if Nixon did not look good on camera, it was that his heavy beard, which no makeup can completely hide, and his general appearance after his recent illness, simply were no match for Mr. Kennedy's well-known photogenic qualities. Nor were the cameramen anything but professionally impartial. What defeated the Vice President were two major tactical errors, a violation of an ancient political rule: Never add to the stature of your opponent; and bad timing of the broadcast.

Here was Senator Kennedy, at that time virtually unknown, locked in highly visible combat with a man familiar to everyone, through the office he held, his many public appearances, and his constant presence in the news. To the public, it was David against Goliath, the young comer against the established professional, and there could be no doubt whose side they would take. Moreover, with every appearance on the screen the professional was giving national exposure to the unknown challenger, who could never have reached so large an audience with so much impact if it had not been for the debates and the tremendous public interest they attracted. Nixon's error, which may have been a prime factor in his loss of the election, was compounded by something over which he had no control, that is, his unfortunate faculty of giving the audience the impression that he is not interested in anyone but himself.

What has all this to do with the real merits of a candidate, one may ask? Would Nixon have made a better President than Kennedy? Would any other candidate, given the same set of circumstances, done any better in the White House? We shall never know. Television was the powerful determining factor. President Kennedy's photogenic qualities, his David-and-Goliath debates with Nixon, and the Vice President's tactical errors—all these conspired to subvert any real debate on the actual merits of the men, or their ability to deal with the issues of our time. It was, as most observers now agree, the first election to be decided by television.

I believe this to be the really dangerous aspect of television in its relation to politics. It obscures, if it does not actually overwhelm, the facts about the issues in any campaign by giving the candidate who makes the best visual impact on the voters a powerful advantage. While the medium exposes weakness or deceit in a candidate, the opposite side of that coin is its tendency to exalt personality. Nixon was at his best in Moscow, arguing with Nikita Khrushchev over the merits of capitalism and communism, in a model kitchen at a trade fair. At home, talking to his own people on television, he was at his worst.

Even more dangerous, perhaps, is that a medium so influential politically as television should also be so costly, to the point where only the rich can afford it. This has been the final thrust of a trend which has grown in dimensions during the twentieth century, a time when the getting and keeping of high public office has become so expensive that it is now the province of the rich. If the candidates themselves are not rich, they must surround themselves with rich supporters. This may not be necessarily a bad thing as long as the men of wealth are also men of integrity acting honestly in the public interest. We have been fortunate to have had so many of them. But the danger that this may not always be so is a clear and present one. As matters stand, we are defenseless against the man who has almost unlimited personal resources, or who is in a position to raise large sums, and who knows how to use television as the highly effective weapon it can be.

Nor can we easily contemplate turning the election of candidates over to advertising agencies employing television, as some candidates seem to suggest, and in fact are already doing in a limited way. The agencies, who would rather have a can than a candidate, are experts in manipulating the truth to serve the client—in this case the man who seeks office. They are adept in the creation of phony attitudes, and in adding phony dimensions to an otherwise clear-cut issue. For them, issues are resolved through the soothing ministrations of lies of value rather than the blatant lies of fact.

I propose a remedy for this condition. It will not be a popular remedy as far as the politicians and the broadcasters are concerned, and I can imagine all sorts of objections raised to it. Nevertheless, I submit it as a step in the proper direction, if nothing more. I propose that each candidate for the Presidency be given two hours of network time free, on all three networks simultaneously—and no more, except in case of a national emergency. This pattern of allotment could also be carried out on a state and local level as well. The candidate would be free to use the time in any kind of division he cared to make—that is, four half-hour appearances, or two-hour segments, or whatever seemed best for his purposes. But two hours would be the limit. The public would be spared hours of oratory. The networks would no longer be harassed by the problem of equal time. The candidates would get the undivided attention of the voters for a specific period, no more or less than the others, and so the rich candidate could not overwhelm the less affluent one. The late Senator Robert Kennedy was in agreement with me. During his Indiana primary campaign in May 1968, he charged in an interview with Walter Cronkite, of CBS, that the broadcasters were getting rich out of political campaigns and suggested that candidates be given free time.

If we do not have some fair and equitable arrangement soon, it seems obvious that national politics will end up in the hands of America's multimillionaire families, who may or may not use their power in the interest of the public.

Before we can come to so sensible a solution, it may be that more illusions may have to be dispelled about television and what it is capable of doing or not doing. One of the most persistent myths, for example, is that the television camera cannot editorialize, that it only reproduces what it sees. But what it sees is selectively manipulated by the director, and sometimes the emphasis can be changed cleverly by editing the sound track as well. To cite a not uncommon instance, if television is covering political appearances by competing candidates, when the edited film is shown on the screen it may let the viewer hear one candidate make a point, followed by prolonged, tumultuous applause, after which the second candidate is heard, to be greeted only by a quickly cut-off burst of cheers and applause. Thus applause is selectively edited sometimes, to make it appear that one candidate was greeted with considerably more enthusiasm than the other. Or again, one man may be seen longer and to better advantage on the screen. If such editing has any virtue at all, it may eliminate some of the synthetic enthusiasm produced by the claques the candidates bring to the halls.

Another difficulty about understanding television and its effect on politics lies in thinking about listeners as a mass audience. The candidate may be addressing five thousand people in a packed hall, but so far as the television viewer is concerned, he is talking most often to a man and his wife sitting in their living room. This puts the knowledgeable candidate in something of a dilemma. Should he address the live audience, employing all the usual oratorical techniques designed for a large number of people gathered in a large place? His presence there gives him virtually no option. Yet he may be acutely conscious that a far larger audience is seeing him on television, and this home audience's reactions may be quite different. Perhaps candidates would be better advised not to try to embrace both audiences at once.

There seems to be a prevalent notion that it is necessary for a candidate to give some kind of performance when he appears on the tube, as though he were in show business. He ought to keep it firmly in mind that television is only another means of communicating with people. Those who attempt to give a performance are convicted of rank amateurism on sight.

Ultimately, of course, television's true importance politically is its influence on the Presidency. As matters stand, this vital factor is in the hands of the owners of the medium. Surely it is not too much to say that the importance of the man who occupies the White House in these times is so great that his selection cannot be left to the unfettered whims of a medium that uses the public air for private profit.

*The Network Managements:*

It is not often that the proprietors of large corporations are compelled to admit in public that their left hand doesn't know what the right is doing, but this opportunity presented itself to the network that sponsored *The $64,000 Question* in the investigation following the disclosure that the quiz program had been rigged, along with others of the same genre.

In hearings before the Federal Communications Commission, officials of the network testified categorically that they did not know, nor did the officers of the company know, about the massive dishonesty which had been perpetrated on one of the largest viewing audiences television has ever drawn. This astounding declaration was taken on faith by the examiners, at least publicly, but in the broadcasting business there were many who found it difficult, at least, to believe.

One can only admire, in a perverse way, the sublime arrogance of these officials. They were asking the public to believe that, as co-producers of this program with the independent organization which formulated it, they did not know contestants were given the answers, instructed to dramatize their agonized groping for answers on the air, and were paid what amounted to a bribe for doing so, when ostensibly they were to get only what they won on the program. By an absurd mockery of justice, some of those who took the bribes were prosecuted, but many people in and out of broadcasting thought the wrong people had been taken to court.

Certainly by the most elementary considerations of right and wrong, those who offered the bribes were equally guilty, and so were the network officials. Yet these officials blandly declared they knew nothing about the whole thing, which was equivalent to saying they did not know what was happening, in the most fundamental way, in their own business. This was particularly odd in view of the fact that the rigging of the shows was widely known and discussed in every studio in town while they were on. It would have been an innocent broadcaster indeed who did not know in those days that quiz shows were crooked. Even if it could be believed that top officials of the networks were so immersed in corporate matters that they did not know what was happening in the programing department, there were unquestionably people in every network in responsible positions who did know.

That there is a fundamental weakness in network managements is also evidenced by the rapidity and frequency with which they change some officers. The descent from genius to bum is often accomplished with startling speed. One day the president of a network is acclaimed as the man responsible for the organization's present leadership.

Then the ratings begin to slip a little, and it turns out that there are fatal flaws in the president's character which no one seemed to have noticed before, and he disappears from public view—quietly, the public relations people hope, in a dignified flurry of regretful letters, but occasionally in an unconstructive blaze of recrimination.

Sometimes an official is widely known in the industry as a man who has been handing producing commitments to his friends, for a reasonable percentage of the profits, and perhaps is on the take in other respects, but these unpalatable facts seldom get out of the industry. The general public only knows that another of the captains and kings has departed, and may not realize even that much unless some evidences of executive-suite mayhem and skulduggery slip out from under the carpet into the headlines.

These descents from virtue, and accompanying intramural wars, would not be important if the network officers did not possess so much power through the medium they control. The power is implicit not only in what is seen on the tube, but in the simple possession of so much money. The networks gross $2,200,000,000 annually. That much money in the hands of a relatively small number of people, no matter who they are, represents enormous power—socially, politically, and in every other way. People with such power should be required to read Lord Acton frequently.

What happens to network profits? Partly they go to finance lobbies in Washington, where the interests of the networks are advanced in Congress, whose members are often invited to help protect them from the Federal Communications Commission. Four men represent the networks in Washington. Only one of them is a registered lobbyist, but the others are in more or less constant operation on the Hill, and no one is under any illusion about what they are doing. The American Broadcasting Company is represented by Alfred Beckman. The National Broadcasting Company has two men, "Scoop" Russell, an old friend of General Sarnoff; and Peter Kenney, a vice-president of NBC who is the only registered lobbyist of the broadcasting group. The Columbia Broadcasting System has Theodore Koop.

Nor is this the extent of the networks' lobbying and general propaganda efforts. The National Association of Broadcasters, an organization which is maintained, in effect, by the networks, is a trade association with a powerful voice in media other than the electronic. There is also the Office of Radio and Television Information, an offshoot of the NAB, which acts as a public relations agency, preparing the institutional advertising which lists the few hours of culture, or pretenses to culture, which the networks offer every month; putting out press releases advancing the interests of the broadcasters; and publicizing the results of polls, sometimes paid for by the industry, proving conclusively that broadcasting leads all the other media in whatever is being surveyed.

In network advertising, much is made of broadcasting's "public service." Similarly network managements give eloquent lip service to the cause of public television. But again the left hand seems to be unaware of the activities of the right, or at least there is a surprising lack of communication between them. While CBS, for example, was offering money to help finance the experimental Public Broadcast Laboratory, its lobbyists were joining those of the other networks in trying to kill the bill then before Congress, since passed, creating a Public Broadcasting authority. They did this by the simple expedient of urging the passage of an amendment which would have prohibited any program on public television that might be construed as entertainment.

The broadcasting lobbyists did not succeed with that maneuver, but they are remarkably effective most of the time in selling their point of view to willing congressmen, some of whom own or have interests in broadcasting stations. Anyone who has ever testified before a Congressional committee on anything involving broadcasting knows the astonishment of discovering that a small army of people will appear to dispute his testimony if he is likely to say anything against the industry—and these people will be directly or indirectly connected with the networks.

He will also be sharply reminded of the point I made earlier in these pages—that there is no public control over these networks, and they are free to use their immense power as they choose. Even the smallest of them, ABC, represents a total annual revenue of approximately $575 million, as of 1967.

The strength of the network enterpreneurs was succinctly expressed in 1965 by Ashbrook P. Bryant, chief of the Office of Network Study of the FCC, in the Second Interim Report made by his group, on Television Network Program Procurement. "At present," Bryant wrote in the foreword to that Report, "there appears to be what at least approaches a three-pronged 'oligopoly' of network managers which controls not only economics but, in large measure, art and creativity in television programing. This, the staff believes, hampers the competitive development of the industry toward its maximum, realizable potential of public service.

"A commercial monopoly or 'oligopoly,' if unregulated in the public interest is, of course, inconsistent with and perhaps highly damaging to our system of free competitive enterprise. The staff has concluded that an overcentralization in network managers of economic and creative control over what the American public may see and hear presently exists in television—the most powerful and pervasive of mass communications media. If that conclusion is correct, such an 'oligopoly' would be doubly damaging as it would tend not only to restrict economics but to stultify the creativity and flow of the information and ideas which constitute a significant part of the 'raw materials' from which public opinion and attitudes are produced."

At another point the Interim Report observes: "There is no statutory requirement that network managers take account of the criteria imposed on station licensees in conforming their program schedules to the public interest. Network managers, nonetheless, from the beginning have 'voluntarily' assumed the 'obligation' to provide a program schedule diversified and balanced to meet the needs and interests of the national audience. . . . So it can be seen that all three national television networks have articulated policies which, if adequately carried out, should certainly go a long way in the direction of effectuating the responsibility they have voluntarily assumed to provide a diverse and balanced program schedule designed to serve the various significant tastes and appetites for television service of the national television audience.

"In actual practice, however, the accomplishment of those policies has been—and continues to be—affected by other policies and practices of the networks, advertisers and program producers which directly affect the network television program process."

Exactly. Further, the networks consider it their privilege to practice this kind of manipulation of their license to benefit themselves rather than the public interest, to which they give little more than lip service. It seems not to occur to them that they have been given the privilege of using the public air, and that they have a responsibility to use it for something more than private profit.

The networks enjoy a major advantage from the fact that they are always in a seller's market. Consider the man who wants to publish a newspaper, which he has every right to do. If the paper is a failure, he can and will close it down. If it is successful, he will probably increase the number of pages. The equivalent action on television is to increase the number of hours of transmission in a day. There are five hours of prime time available every day to broadcasters, from 6 to 11 P.M., with the exception of Sunday, when programing is adapted to the fact that many people may be doing something social outside the home. But six days of prime time means that there are 95 hours available for each of the three networks, and so they can sell 285 hours collectively, for higher rates than are charged at other times. With this relatively small amount of time available, in comparison with the number of people who want to buy it, the networks are forever in a seller's market. They are in the fortunate position of being able to say no, and they do.

But the networks will not sell their time without selling the talent too, if they can, and this is where their control and its consequent power exists. Sponsors who want to get on the network's prime time must be prepared to give up their rights.

The networks quite naturally want to keep it that way. They will do anything they can to prevent anyone from intruding on their control of both time and talent. Thus Dr. Frank Stanton, head of CBS, assured Congress, and apparently convinced them, that if the networks had been the sole producers of the quiz programs, instead of only selling the time, as they did in that instance, the scandals would never have happened. This, however, is no answer to the fact that it was common knowledge in the industry that the quiz shows were fixed. The networks must surely have known. If their managers did know, they were as much participants in the fraud as the contestants who took the money and faked their appearances. If they did not know, the conclusion is inescapable that they were inadequate managers.

Perhaps what Dr. Stanton was really saying could be translated even more simply. The quiz scandals would not have happened if we controlled programing as well as the sale of time, he seemed to say, but since we didn't, we're washing our hands of the whole thing. In brief, the networks want the monopoly, the "oligopoly" they already enjoy.

We have been fighting monopoly for a very long time in this country, since the days of Theodore Roosevelt's trust-busting. Legislation has been enacted from time to time to curb it, notably the Sherman Anti-Trust Act, which the Justice Department appears to be enforcing successfully in some quarters, but less successfully in others. Restraints have been placed on the trend toward overpowering bigness in America, but somehow the networks seem to have escaped their effects. Everyone knows there is no such thing as a little monopoly, that can go unnoticed because it is not flagrant enough to come within the obvious purview of the law. The network oligopoly may be only a step toward true monopoly, but it is a long step. The networks began taking it in the days of radio when, through the Artists' Bureau, they began to monopolize both time and talent. What has happened in television is only an extension, and a far more dangerous one, of an established monopolistic practice.

Who *are* these men, we might ask, who control so much money and are capable of wielding so much political and social influence? They are sophisticated, articulate gentlemen, removed from the usual corporate type, whose concentration is so fiercely intent on the great game of business they are all playing. The network entrepreneurs are in that game too, obviously, but they are also in show business, and in one way or another they are involved with all creative arts. Furthermore, they live in close proximity to the news, and what their properties do is profoundly affected by the day-to-day shape of events, where the ordinary business responds customarily to long-range trends. When a President is assassinated, a network not only turns its whole operation over to the news, but it has numerous immediate adjustments it must make in relation to its customers, the sponsors, whose interests are momentarily subordinated to the news and who must be compensated. No other business is so closely attuned to events, not even the other communications media.

Conversely, when the sponsor's interests are paramount, which is nearly all the time, he must be given the largest audience possible, which means mass entertainment —or show business. The network managers, then, are men outside the ordinary confines of corporate management. They constitute a powerful force both inside and outside the structure of American business.

Can anything be done to curb their power and direct the networks toward the public interest? Much can be done, of course, and I have a practical suggestion as a start toward more complete reform. This idea, however, would accomplish a great deal in its own right. I suggest that 50 percent of the programing on television in prime time should be done by independent producers, not by network television. These independents would produce for the advertisers, buying their time from the networks in the customary way. The networks, therefore, would not participate in this programing in any way, except to sell the time. Once removed from the dictation of the networks, one hopes, these prime hours would be free to offer far more diversity and imaginative programing than the networks seem able to provide. In brief, this is a move to divorce content from carrier, which the Department of Justice has long been doing in other entertainment areas, as I shall point out in the next chapter.

I realize that this proposal will be regarded with absolute horror by the network managers. It is exactly what they have done their best in Washington and elsewhere to avoid. Yet if we are going to avert monopoly and do something to channel television more truly toward the public interest, I see no better beginning in sight. And if war it must be, let it begin here.

*The Department of Justice:*

On their successful battle to retain control of both time and talent, the networks have somehow contrived to exempt themselves from the numerous actions taken against other segments of the entertainment business by the Department of Justice, designed to prevent such monopoly. The list of those actions is long, and they have affected vaudeville booking, theater control, radio time and talent, motion picture exhibition, and such oligopolies as the Music Corporation of America represented before the government took action against it.

The Department's purpose has been plain in all these actions—the dissociation of content from carrier, as the legal phrasing goes. In television, time represents the carrier, talent the content. But where consent decrees have ended monopolistic practices, or at least curbed them everywhere else, all attempts to bring identical situations in television to the attention of the Department of Justice have failed. The Department's strange attitude toward these attempts has discouraged those who sponsored them.

If anyone doubts that there is something in television for the government to move against, he need only take a closer look at what the Federal Communications Commission itself describes as "virtual domination of television program markets," and see what it means to the actor, and indeed to all creative groups. The networks' tripartite monopoly permits complete control of casting, and of salaries to be paid to everyone except the biggest stars. It not only permits but encourages the placing of ceilings on what is paid to artists, and there is no doubt that the heads of the monopoly could, at any given moment, agree among themselves on salary cuts for talent.

The FCC has been well aware of this monopoly and its effects. It has duly noted the marked tendency to centralize in network corporations the control of what the American people may see and hear on television, and thus hamper the competitive development of diverse sources for television program service. Here we have an exact reversal of that "condition of competition" within the framework of service in the public interest which had been intended as the principal criterion of program choice under the American system of broadcasting. "It is not desirable," the FCC has said forthrightly, "for so few entities to have such a degree of power with respect to what the American public may see and hear over so many television stations."

Independent program producers also have no doubt about what network monopoly means. They are compelled to deal with the television networks on network terms, or give up all hope of producing programs for exhibition on the networks.

When the FCC proposed that a portion of prime time be given over to independent programs not owned by the networks, they responded with a barrage of propaganda insulting to the intelligence of those in the business. If the networks did not program all the time on television, they asserted blandly, there would be a blackout on the air and the public would be left looking at blank screens—not an entirely unattractive prospect for many of those numbed by current programing. But there was no truth in this assertion, no more than there was in equally exotic flights into fantasy conceived by the industry's public relations helpers.

The power of the broadcasters extends to the floor of Congress itself, where both senators and representatives either own stations or represent them as lawyers. In 1965, there were nine senators and fourteen representatives in the 89th Congress who had either a direct or a family-related interest in United States broadcasting stations, according to the FCC. There were seventeen Democrats and six Republicans on the list. Fifteen states were represented, with North Carolina appearing four times, Missouri and Virginia three times, and New York twice. President Johnson's broadcasting interests, held through his wife, are well known.

Some members of Congress, it must be said, are not afraid to attack network monopoly forthrightly. In June 1967, when Representative John Moss, of California, introduced a bill providing that a network could not own more than 50 percent of the programs telecast during prime time, he drew up a melancholy rollcall of legislation proposed in the wake of the quiz-show scandals to regulate networks in the public interest. Bills were introduced in the House for such a purpose early in the 86th Congress, and again in the 87th Congress, at about the same time the Senate was producing its own bill to amend the Communications Act to provide for the regulation of networks. Extensive hearings were held by the FCC and by committees of Congress, all of which proved without doubt what everyone in the business already knew—that more than 90 percent of television programs broadcast during prime time were owned or controlled by the originating networks, and that independent producers could not get their programs telecast unless they agreed to give 50 percent or more of the profits to the network, and also, depending on the bargaining, possibly all the syndication rights, both foreign and domestic—not to mention editorial control.

Needless to say, nothing came of any of these bills or hearings, and Representative Moss, in 1967, could only demand rhetorically: "What kind of a system is it that depends on financial payoffs instead of the needs and requirements of the viewing public as to what shall be shown on the public airwaves? The networks apparently look upon the public airwaves as a giant money tree to be shaken until all but a few barren leaves are left as a token."

If this were not enough for the Department of Justice to base an action upon, there are exercises of network power equally monopolistic in their effect. The oligopoly is perfectly capable, for example, of ending the economic life of any individual who depends for his living on television, and who has been unfortunate enough to have displeased the network bosses. There is no recourse for such a banned individual. He cannot demonstrate the existence of a conspiracy, because the networks will simply fall back upon their sellers' market alibi: There is a shortage of time, and therefore not enough work for everybody.

Ironically, the networks scream "Rape!" whenever there is any threat of censorship imposed on them from the outside, yet they have established their own powerful censorship, not simply in programing, but against those who have displeased them. At one time the Black List was political, although the networks calmly denied what everyone knew to be true—that those who had been involved with communist-front organizations, either innocently or by conviction, or who had signed petitions supporting them, or who had even been suspected of left-wing sympathies found it difficult or impossible to get on the air. The degree of their banishment depended on the publicity generated by the original offense, then or later, but it was usually total. In these cases, the network managements supinely yielded not only to pressure from the advertising agencies, representing their conservative sponsors, which could be expected, but to every right-wing organization with a list and a typewriter as well.

While this kind of black-listing is bad enough, in both a moral and a legal sense, it is no worse than the kind of arrogant censorship still existing, in which the black list has been extended to cover all those whom the networks dislike for any reason, particularly those who oppose them, by testifying at hearings, making public pronouncements in the press, or writing magazine articles. One or two offenders have been permitted to escape punishment by recanting, after which they are graciously allowed to work again.

Thus the networks carry on their perpetual war against the real public interest, while Congress frets and does little, the FCC is divided against itself, and the Department of Justice adopts a calm view of obvious monopoly. When a citizen takes it upon himself to oppose the monolith, he is crushed by another monolith, the American legal structure. Five years ago, in California, a man instituted an anti-trust suit against the networks. It took him four years to get the networks' lawyers into court for a preliminary hearing, and after a time, faced with the prospect of more years of delay and consequent expense—important to him but trifling to the networks—he gave up and withdrew the action.

If the Department of Justice is to protect us against the concentration of power in any industry, which it is charged by law to do, it is difficult to see how it can ignore much longer the immense power held by networks, economically, socially, politically, and in every other way. Certainly we need protection from such power, and government is the only force large enough to curb the networks. But it must be government with sufficient political guts to stand up to the crude blackmail practiced by the network lobbies, which have terrified potentially recalcitrant legislators by the mere hint of the power television holds over them, too. The implication —and it is crystal clear to the lawmaker—is that in the next election, when he is fighting for his continued existence in public life, television and radio will either give him the deadly blow of silence, sometimes sufficient in itself, or it may take more or less subtle action against him in its news coverage of the campaign, employing its celebrated expertise in filming and editing.

The Department of Justice needs to take to heart the damning indictment of television set forth by Ashbrook P. Bryant, whose characterization of it as a powerful oligopoly has already been cited. It must be clear by now, even to the most reluctant government agency, that this oligopoly is both damaging to and inconsistent with the public interest.

*The Network News Departments:*

One of the more deplorable mistakes of the American public, where communications are concerned, is its belief that reading the headlines constitutes knowledge of what is going on. Headline reading, self-evidently, is only partial knowledge, and a small part at that. Yet millions of Americans satisfy themselves with this fragmentary portion of the news.

Radio and television networks encourage and fortify the practice. The newspaper headline reader gets his five-minute capsules of news every hour on the hour and half hour, and considers himself informed. News takes a little longer on television. The insertion of film clips into what the announcer is reading (essentially little more than the five-minute radio broadcast) stretches the time to fifteen minutes, minus four minutes or so for commercials. It is possible to stretch the fifteen minutes to a half hour by adding to the mixture a little more film, two or three capsule interviews, a smattering of the trivialities known as feature material, and perhaps something of that strangled form of self-expression described as commentary that is editorializing suffering from emasculation.

To the viewer who already contents himself with headline reading and five-minute wrapups on radio, the fifteen-minute or half-hour television show seems like a veritable fountain of information. The networks have been able to offer newspapers formidable competition, and indeed are in the process of changing their character, by being first with the news, on both television and radio. Unfortunately, the speed of delivery has obscured a fundamental truth, that there is no relation between speed and the quality of what is being transmitted, nor for that matter between speed and validity. Speed, in fact, improves neither.

The headline reader finds it easy to believe that network editors and reporters are giving him what they think he wants to read, or should read, but somehow it never occurs to him that when he is watching a news show he is looking at show business. Even without Ed Sullivan, or a quizmaster, or a "host," it is still show business. Those sincere, buttoned-down figures on the screen, with their characteristic façade of bluff honesty, or boyish charm, or affectations of pouting skepticism, are jugglers and comics, actors of the news, portraying dramatically what has often been written by someone else. Some radio and television personalities on network news or "commentary" programs have even acquired reputations as great reporters, notwithstanding that they have never done anything resembling reporting but to walk into the studio and read or recite from memory what has been written for them.

What passes for "in depth" reporting on the networks is usually appallingly superficial. Occasionally, in a documentary, the reporters not only get beneath the surface, which many of them are capable of doing, but are allowed to present what they find with at least a semblance of truth. It is distressingly easy for them to slip over the line, however. In these cases the story, and often the program, mysteriously disappears. Such was the case with David Brinkley when, on his own half-hour show, he exposed the shocking corruption of the Federal road-building program, with its broad highways leading into nowhere, in one instance, and accompanying evidences of money siphoned off into bottomless pockets to the tune of millions upon millions of dollars. His interview with the Federal administrator of the highway program may have been one of the most embarrassing episodes involving a public figure ever seen on the tube. Apparently it was too embarrassing. The program was canceled soon afterward, with the usual bland excuse, and nothing more was ever heard again on the air about the corruption. It would be a naïve observer indeed who would not conclude that the networks had retreated willingly before pressure from high places.

While the power inherent in network news reporting, and the abuse of it, would be an important issue at any time, it is particularly vital now, in our era of trouble. This fact was pointed up sharply by George Gent in *The New York Times* on May 19, 1968, as he analyzed the relationship of the tube to dissent.

"There is a real danger," Mr. Gent wrote, "that television may be contributing unwittingly to the growing irrationalism affecting American political and social life. This, at least, would be a reasonable conclusion for anyone watching the medium's coverage of the various movements of dissent in recent weeks. Television, for better or worse, is the way most Americans get their news and form opinions on the events shaping their times. How those events are presented to the TV-viewing public will determine in large measure the nation's response to the challenges facing it. It should be obvious, therefore, that if television is presenting a distorted or superficial image of these forms of social protest, then the American public will respond by either overreacting to these challenges to the status quo or by dismissing them as inconsequential.

"Either response could be disastrous. Certainly there are vital social and moral issues involved in the Negro, student and anti-Vietnam protest movements, but there is much confusion and disharmony in the ranks of the protesters themselves, and it will not serve the public well for television to do no more than mirror that confusion. Unfortunately, that is what it appears to be doing. Indeed, TV can be said to be adding to the confusion by giving voice to the strident dissenters without tackling the much tougher journalistic job of bringing clarity out of what seems to be chaos."

The charge heard most frequently in 1968 was that television had aided and abetted the ghetto riots by carrying airborne seeds of violence across the country into every home or bar where black men could see other black men applying the torch and looting, thus inspiring others to do the same.

While this is not yet a proved case, there is enough known truth in it to have made the networks exert a little caution. The riots in the summer of 1967 were given all-out coverage, while those following the assassination of Martin Luther King, Jr., were approached in a more restrained style. The report of the President's riot commission did not indict television as an inciter of riots, but it did point out that "the question is far-reaching and a sure answer is beyond the range of presently available scientific techniques."

The large question raised by television's relationship to violence, however, is not one that can be quietly shoved under the rug, as the network entrepreneurs would love to do. The fact that it is a complicated question, to which there are no ready answers, does not obviate the responsibility of the proper government agencies to investigate it thoroughly. What happens when union men across the country see strikers in conflict with the police on their television screens? Do these scenes create picket lines elsewhere? No one knows for certain. When the small screen shows black marchers under verbal assault from screaming white racists, or white men, particularly police, battling with black demonstrators, are passions aroused on both sides among the watchers, and does further violence result? When television news programs show a Detroit housewife practicing with her new rifle, does the slight inspire other women to go out and buy guns, anticipating riots?

Some observers of the social scene have said flatly that the power of extreme black militants is in direct proportion to the attention they get from the media. Whitney Young, director of the National Urban League, has asserted that Stokely Carmichael's following consists of "about fifty

Negroes and about 5,000 white newsmen." While the implication of this charge may not be nearly so true in the case of newspapers, certainly television has brought Carmichael's face and voice into millions of homes—with what effect yet remains to be measured.

The large social question raised here has been summarized succinctly by the United States Solicitor General, Erwin Griswold. In a speech at Tulane Law School in April 1968, he observed that: "There may be real room to question whether we have psychologically caught up with the developments in communications speed and distribution, whether we are capable of absorbing and evaluating all of the materials which are now communicated daily to hundreds of millions of people."

The trouble with network television's relationship to news is that it doesn't simply *report* the news. It *presents* the news, and that is no longer journalism. As one TV newsman admitted recently, "We're still basically in show business." An audience looking at violence and action and movement on the tube hour after hour is not going to sit by quietly and watch people talk. Consequently the announcer who reads the news on the air is supplemented by filmed coverage of the events he is describing. In that way, the war in Vietnam has been brought into American living rooms, a coverage which has made its own singular contribution to the national unrest over the conflict. In a more particularized way, the reporting of other kinds of clashes has had an undeniable impact on the nation's consciousness, and here television has sometimes gone far beyond the bounds of honest reporting.

War requires no assist from cameraman or producer. It is sufficiently grim and terrible of itself to make its own point. But other varieties of combat call for show business in the news, as the country has seen in some recent examples. When KNBC, Los Angeles, sent a film team to record a debate on Vietnam at Claremont Men's College, students were indignant when they saw the crew methodically unloading a supply of posters with both pro and con war slogans posted on them. A KNBC "spokesman" remarked later that the posters were only "colorful additions to the set." There have been some other colorful additions since then. A city bus was burned by protesters on cue from TV cameramen. Two hippies blocked President Johnson's entry into a Washington club at the persuasion of another zealous crew. This kind of thing has not yet become the rule, but it is far more common than the public realizes.

Congress has at last been stirred to action by such reports. Early in May 1968, a House Commerce investigations subcommittee opened hearings in Chicago to look into a charge that WBBM-TV, the Columbia Broadcasting System's owned and operated outlet in Chicago, deliberately staged a marijuana party purported to have been held on the Northwestern University campus. After the first two days of the hearing, Representative Harley O. Staggers (D., West Virginia), chairman of the subcommittee, asserted: "According to evidence already received by the subcommittee, the pot party was staged by the station. There is evidence that the party was filmed by the station in a privately owned residence and not university-controlled housing."

There were other implications in the incident as the hearing developed. If the station had indeed staged the party, it had also violated the law in Illinois, where smoking marijuana is illegal, both by handling the weed and by not informing the authorities.

Among the denials entered by the television interests involved, perhaps the most interesting was that of Dr. Frank Stanton, president of CBS, owner of WBBM-TV. "We covered it in the nature of investigative reporting," Dr. Stanton said with a straight face, supporting the station's decision as proper. The purpose of the show, he added, was "to show the nature of the social problem involved in smoking marijuana," according to *The New York Times.*

Another defender, surprising to some who read the account of the hearings, was Newton F. Minow, former chairman of the

Federal Communications Commission, who now appeared wearing a different hat as WBBM's lawyer. It was Mr. Minow, one recalls, who coined that deadly phrase, "vast wasteland," and gave network television a description of itself which no amount of public relations could entirely displace.

It was significant, as hearings developed, that the networks scarcely had a friend in court. The atmosphere of the hearing room was definitely hostile, from committeemen to spectators. There appeared to be a definite feeling that this time television had gone too far, although it had traveled the same distance often enough before.

When the Columbia University riots closed down that institution in April 1968, television relayed the images of violence and rebellion to campuses across the country. Did they inspire the riots and seizure of buildings that immediately took place on many campuses scattered across the land? The possibility, at least, was raised. Grayson Kirk, Columbia's president, well understood the power of television, whatever his failings may have been in not understanding the students. Only a short time before the university was brought to its knees, he talked about the effect of television on politics and remarked: "Our leaders are expected to appear almost on call before the television cameras, to hold innumerable press conferences, and to share their thoughts, even if they may be fragmentary and half-formed, with everyone in the country. No leader can long survive such ordeals and emerge from them unscathed."

Only a few days later, President Kirk himself was facing the television cameras, to be cross-examined by three reporters about the Columbia riots. He had been preceded on other programs by a number of Columbia faculty members and students. One professor, being interviewed off camera, broke down under the stress of emotion. A few minutes later he obligingly broke down again *on* camera.

President Johnson gave somewhat reluctant credit to television's power the day after he announced his decision not to run for re-election. He chose an audience which could hardly have appreciated his words more, a convention of the National Association of Broadcasters. He intimated broadly in his speech that television had played a major role in his decision not to run. "I understand," he said, "far better than some of my severe and intolerant critics will admit, my own shortcomings as a communicator." In the indirect way beloved of politicians, he went on to imply that television's coverage of the Vietnam war had been the force behind much of the public's opposition to his war policies. Television, he said, appeared "better suited to convey the actions of conflict than to dramatizing the words that the leaders use in trying to end the conflict."

The network moguls employ the same kind of rhetoric to defend their war coverage as they do to excuse the Evanston marijuana party, the Los Angeles signboards, and virtually everything else they do. It is all in the public interest. Have the black militants been overexposed? Not at all, according to

Richard Salant, president of CBS News. "Our test is not whether we approve of the event or agree with the individual, but whether it is legitimate news."

One can hardly help wondering about the networks' definition of legitimate news. Do they think the deliberate staging of news is legitimate? If it is true (the issue had not yet been decided as this was written) that a Chicago station arranged a marijuana party for its own benefit, does that come under the head of legitimate news, or even legitimate documentary making? Is the paying of peace marchers by a TV network to stage a parade especially for the camera's benefit —is this, too, legitimate? What price legitimacy!

*The Advertising Agencies:*

Something dreadful happened to American good taste on the day one advertising executive turned to another, and with rapt anticipation of a cat contemplating a piece of kidney, asked a fateful question: "What's wrong with toilet paper?"

The agency answer to that question is, "Nothing, if we can sell it." Television sells it. The medium which shrinks delicately from the kind of female undergarment advertising common in both magazines and newspapers thinks nothing of peddling toilet paper, patent medicines, deodorants, laxatives, indigestion remedies, and other nostrums with the most explicit detail. As

Ernest Hocking observes, "The schools offer courses in ethics and esthetics and, now, a general theory of values. But as consumers of goods, we are constant practitioners of value-judgments, and as constantly in need of teaching."

Professor Hocking goes on to point out a significant fact about our immense advertising bill, "running toward billions and borne, of course, by the consumer." While it beckons us, he says, "to genuine new facilities as well as thrills and ticklings, [it] has become essentially a *bill for falsehood*. Not that advertising lies in regard to facts—this it hesitates to do—its falsities are *lies of emotion*. . . . And my point is that in any civilization *falsehoods of feeling are more deadly than falsehoods of fact*. They are also more insidious; for they are irrefutable—they do not argue, they infect the mind. Are we perhaps becoming an infected people?"

Certainly the infection of the television commercial has passed well beyond the point of being merely insidious. It is bad enough that the volume level of the commercial is raised above that of the remainder of the program (the ear affirms what the network denies), but night and day the commercial is our constant companion on radio and television. At breakfast it reminds us of the peril of halitosis (we will not be kissed); at lunch it warns of B.O. (it prohibits what occurs when the kissing stops); and at dinner it tells us of the imminent danger of irregularity (we will not enjoy what we have just eaten).

It would be unfair to argue, of course, that the makers of toilet paper do not have a right to advertise their product. One only asks that they refrain from unrolling it the length of a football field at mealtime. Nor can it be successfully argued without seeming un-American that cigarette companies should not be permitted to advertise, since Russia is the only country in the world which forbids cigarette advertising. On the other hand, there is ample reason to resent being told constantly, in defiance of the most authoritative medical opinion, that smoking contributes to the health and happiness of the young. Do we really want our sons and daughters to walk a mile for a cancer?

When the false front is stripped away, the advertising agency appears in a somewhat different light than the public usually views it. As essential as advertising may be to the national economy, and to the existence of all the media except books, it occupies an anomalous position. It is an industry predicated on the idea that people should spend their money for goods, whether they need them or not, and regardless of whether the product has any true merit. This idea, of course, is in the interest of the industries it serves. Oddly enough, however, some industries think of the advertising agencies as necessary evils, although others may regard them as absolutely indispensable.

The agency's attitude is that anything and everything is fair game as long as the client is happy, and the agencies believe their clients *will* be happy just as long as they get results for them. Nonetheless, there are irreconcilables who refuse to make a joyful sound. These are advertisers who are not so emotionally involved with their own products that they cannot see the false values being employed to sell them. I know one manufacturer who dislikes his advertising agency so much he sometimes can't remember its name when he wants to refer to it.

But then, the advertising industry is too busy to worry much about these matters of sentiment. It is active now in the business of selling political candidates, with the same enthusiasm and many of the same techniques it has used so successfully to improve the sale of deodorants and toilet paper. A candidate, it has been discovered, can be packaged and sold like any other product to the unsuspecting American consumer. In the Nebraska primary elections of 1968, for example, Governor Ronald Reagan of California, who did not even campaign in the state, nevertheless compiled an astonishing number of votes for the Presidency, although he was not openly running for the office. The impetus for this showing was provided by a skillful series of television commercials in his behalf. Elated with the Nebraska result, the Governor had the films rushed immediately to Oregon and the next primary.

Selling candidates by the advertising agency is not new. It is simply becoming more effective, so that sometimes one has a hard time discerning where a candidate's natural talents for the job, if any, end and where the façade erected by advertising and public relations begins.

If the application of advertising techniques to politics continues at the present rate, it is not hard to visualize an all-purpose commercial in which we see the candidate strolling through a peaceful rural scene, hand in hand with a girl (one old enough to vote, naturally), while the narrator tells us throatily how the aspirant grew up in the land he surveys. "This is [candidate's] country!" the announcer says. From there it is only a step to having him smoke a preferred brand as he walks the fields, until at last we watch him waving happily as he steps into his house, carrying a bar of cleansing soap, a deodorant, and a roll of toilet paper as he vanishes in the direction of the bathroom to freshen up after his hike. Fantasy, to be sure, but the voter should ask himself if he ever thought the time would come when an agency handling a candidate would refer to him as "our political product."

If one applies the falsities, or the "lies of emotion," as Professor Hocking calls them, not only to the candidate but to the issues of a campaign as well, the result can only be appalling. Surely such selling techniques do no real service to the candidate, nor to the country. Yet the fact is that they are being increasingly used, and with effect.

What advertising does, in the case of both candidates and soap, is to project an "image," that word which has become the new American religion. The word itself is a falsity, yet how powerful it has become in our societp! It is now unsafe, or at least unwise, to imply that any group of individuals likely to write letters is anything less than exemplary, or that it ever acts from any except the noblest motives. This includes the United States itself, as far as school textbooks are concerned. In the same way, the image of the candidate is projected by advertising and public relations experts. What the nature of the real man may be, the voter does not know until he gets into office. Then, in spite of the most highly professional efforts to keep on projecting the image, the truth inevitably begins to emerge under the pressure of events.

When an advertising agency is selling a product, in the normal course of commerce, it is not concerned with the relationship of the product to society. Its concern is to sell whatever is being sold in sufficient quantity to please the manufacturer enough so that he will continue to retain the agency. No agency employs a man to evaluate the dangers of a program in its relation to the social, economic, or political structure of the country. It is not surprising, consequently, that there is the same unconcern for the public welfare when the product is a political candidate.

Obviously, selling candidates on television is a clear and present danger to the society we live in, but it is not the only damage to the fabric of our life which advertising on the tube represents. The ubiquitous commercial itself, assaulting our ears in steadily increasing quantity, is a massive leveler of taste, a noisy irritant adding to the din about us.

Consider the essential nature of the commercial, if you will. It asks us to believe in an unreal world, further adding to the dangerous confusion between illusion and reality which is the curse of our time. Loudly, insistently, it proclaims that we are all likely to be loved if only we use a product that will make us smell better, shape our hair, mold our figures, make our teeth gleam, or otherwise improve our physical structure. Nothing about loving people for themselves. Television advertising, like all advertising, sells the cult of youth and beauty, without which the viewer can be sure he is not likely to be an object of sexual attention, nor has a chance to exist as a happy individual.

The commercial also wants us to believe happiness lies in the beer we drink, the cigarette we smoke, or the car we drive. By a thousand subtle devices, the possession of these things is linked to the good life, until we can scarcely help feeling hopelessly deprived until they are ours. The commercial sells excitement, thrills, sex, acceptance by others, the joys of affluence—a bright, ebullient world in which there are no real problems except how to get the wash cleaner, or to put something on the table the children will eat as though they had been starving. We know the reality is far different from what we see; the viewer has only to move his eyes away from the tube to observe the world as it is. But why make the effort to deal with real problems when it is so much better to sit back and let the glowing screen create a world in which everything is fresh and clean and beautiful?

One of the most deadly ironies perpetuated by the commercial is the linking of vibrant life with unacknowledged death. The lovely girls walking hand in hand with their handsome men through splendid rural scenery, thrusting their chiseled profiles into the wind, soaking up the glories of nature—

and holding in their hands the slender white instrument of death, while the announcer assures us that this is the sure path to contentment. Ah yes, come back to cancer country, to heart-attack land, where every prospect pleases and only the commercial is vile.

Indignant at the assault of the television commercial on our sensibilities, our taste, our intelligence, on truth itself, we look vainly for some sense of responsibility on the part of the agencies for what they are doing. Instead, there is only contempt for those who dare to protest. They are eggheads, or enemies of the American free enterprise system, or dangerous radicals. Moreover, many advertising executives deny with the passionate sincerity of one whose pocketbook is threatened that there is anything wrong with what the commercials do. The networks' excuse is that the commercials make it possible for them to bring us the great world of entertainment in living color that we should all be grateful for instead of complaining about.

It is plain, then, that nothing can be expected from either source in the way of voluntary reform. If it ever comes, reform will be the product of an aroused viewing audience, unable to take any more—or alternatively, an audience that will slowly, silently melt away on the rating charts until all that remains, like the Cheshire cat, is a toothpaste smile and a smoke ring.

*People Who Take The Ratings Seriously:*

As everyone in and out of broadcasting knows by this time, television lives by the audience measurements provided by a dozen or so rating services, of which two or three are pre-eminent. On their reports of who is looking at what, advertising appropriations are determined and shows continue or disappear. Ratings are God in the broadcasting theology. If the reports indicate that a show is not attracting a viable percentage of audience, nothing can save it, no matter what its other merits may be. Conversely, if a show attracts high ratings, nothing can kill it no matter how appalling it is, even in the opinion of those involved with it.

That the essential insanity of this system is taken seriously may be considered as a measurement of another kind. By and large, it is *not* taken seriously by anyone except those who have a vested interest in it. The audience measurers take *themselves* very seriously indeed, and not only because they run a business which brings them power and money; they regard themselves as the savants of a new science. The advertising people and the network managers take the system seriously because they have no other choice. They have carefully locked themselves into it, and they say there is no escape.

Audience measuring is not, however, the more or less exact science its entrepreneurs claim it to be. Indeed, grave doubts have been raised about its accuracy. Even the basic premise upon which ratings are predictated is seriously open to question. The fact that a man looks at a program is no proof whatever that he likes either the program or the product it advertises. But the adoration of statistics is so profound in

America that mere numbers are considered proof of approval.

There are other reasons why the ratings may be less than accurate. The small size of the sample is one, and sometimes there is good reason to believe that there has been inaccurate or incomplete reporting of viewing data. In the case of fixed panels, whose reactions to programs are sampled to make the report, there is the possibility that such panels have been conditioned in various ways, or their aging may have also changed their viewpoints. Some samples, furthermore, exclude various parts of the country. Agencies can be accused of not doing their field work properly, or of improperly editing and weighting their procedures. It happens, too, that some households selected for inclusion in a sample do not cooperate.

When network people are confronted by accumulated evidence that programs rise or fall by virtue of a system of highly doubtful validity, they shrug their shoulders and say, "We live by the ratings. There isn't any other way." And they say this in spite of widespread skepticism in their own ranks, and in advertising agencies, about the worth of statistics on which the spending of millions of dollars is based, not to mention determining the kind of viewing millions of people will be permitted.

The government is not unaware of this problem. In a report of the Committee on Interstate and Foreign Commerce in January 1966, its members pointed out that they had exposed rigged quiz shows and payola, and similarly, they said, "false or misleading audience measurement ratings must be exposed."

The report continued: "Rightly or wrongly, sponsors react to the audience rating systems. Millions of dollars turn on the rating levels. The immediate and long-range future of all types of programs—news reports, mysteries, comedies, westerns, etc. —are controlled by the ratings which each show receives. If this rating system is to continue we must make certain that the rating received is the rating achieved—no more, and no less.

"If public reaction is an appropriate measure, then the public reaction should be free from any tampering or adjustment for private purposes. If public surveys are to be used to determine where, when, and what will be broadcast, we must assure that such surveys are not misused.

"The broadcasting industry as a whole shares this responsibility. Fortunately, a number of responsible business interests are aware of this and share the view that the reliability of audience measurement techniques and the proper use of audience measurement results constitute an important aspect of broadcasting in the public interest."

Certainly the public interest will not be served if the investigation of ratings is left to the network management. As the Report observes further, commenting on research of the measurements business already undertaken, "It can be stated without any reservation that none of the programs described above would have been undertaken if it had not been for the investigations and hearings conducted by the subcommittee and the insistence on the part of the subcommittee following the hearings that remedial action be instituted. . . . Improvements in the broadcast rating picture which have been made in the last 3 years have been due primarily, if not entirely, to the investigations and proceedings conducted by this subcommittee. If these efforts have improved not only ratings but, indirectly at least, have resulted in making broadcasters more responsible in the conduct of their licensed activities, the time and effort spent by the subcommittee have been well worthwhile."

But one can hardly take an optimistic view of what, in the long run, has been accomplished. As the subcommittee noted, it took government action to produce any move at all on the part of the industry to improve ratings procedures, and the melancholy fact is that all of the industry's subsequent attempts at improvement have failed.

It may be that reform has been approached in the wrong way. Until we get a rating system which registers the viewer's disgust as well as his approbation, very little faith can be placed in audience measurement by whatever device. Who knows how many shows with high ratings are viewed out of boredom, habit, or because there is nothing else worth looking at just at that time? Why look at a program simply because its rating is higher than another's?

Somehow the tyranny of the ratings must be abolished. If the networks are their willing or unwilling prisoners, we, the viewers, must consider it our duty to liberate them.

*The Board of Public Television:*

Among the many millions of words, the thousands of books, pamphlets, articles, and newspaper stories about television, the Report of the Carnegie Commission on Educational Television stands out like the landmark it is. This stimulating document is called "Public Television: A Program for Action," and its effectiveness was proved almost immediately with the passage by Congress of the Public Television Act, a historic piece of legislation that would probably not even have been introduced, much less enacted, if the Report had not been written.

Passage of the Act is an even greater tribute to the pressure generated by the Report when one considers the extraordinary effort made by the networks' lobby to block it. I have mentioned earlier what was perhaps their most outrageous maneuver—an effort to insert a clause in the bill which would have prohibited anything approaching entertainment from being broadcast on public television—but this was only one of the ways in which they tried either to kill or emasculate the bill.

Like many other people concerned about the medium, I was surprised and pleased by the quality of the Board which President Johnson appointed to direct the affairs of the Public Television Corporation. They were men who, one could be sure, well understand the difference between public and educational television, which the Carnegie Report had so ably defined. I have earlier described that difference briefly, but the Commission's definition is worth repeating:

"Commercial television," says the Report, "seeks to capture the large audience;

it relies mainly upon the desire to relax and to be entertained. Instructional television lies at the opposite end of the scale; it calls upon the instinct to work, build, learn, and improve, and asks the viewer to take on responsibilities in return for a later reward. Public television, to which the Commission has devoted its major attention, includes all that is of human interest and importance which is not at the moment appropriate or available for support by advertising, and which is not arranged for formal instruction."

In recognizing these differences, the Report confirmes that the function of entertainment can also be educational, in the best sense of the word. For in the end—is it not true?—nothing appears on the screen which does not "educate" the viewer in one way or another, for better or worse.

Having passed the Act, Congress is now confronted with the problem of how the proposed system of public television it has created. Various schemes have been proposed. My strong endorsement would go to a franchise tax on the sale of time or content by the networks. I would expect this to be a continuing tax, with the money allocated by Congress to public television, and it would be levied on *gross sales* of time and content. A tax of only 3.5 percent would be sufficient to raise the millions of dollars needed to finance public television, an exceedingly small percentage when one considers the enormous earnings of the networks.

If such a tax were levied, the networks would then be performing a real public service, of the kind they are constantly and erroneously proclaiming they are now rendering. They would be returning a little to the public of what it has given them in terms of power and profit for the privilege of using the public air.

Naturally, we may presume that the networks will do everything they can to prevent such a tax, or indeed any other plan by which the networks might contribute to the the financing of public broadcasting. They will argue in the first instance that such a tax would increase the cost of television to their advertisers, but in fact that increase would be too negligible to be significant. It is also better than another kind of proposed tax, one on the license of the manufacturer to make television sets, because the time-and-content tax would be a more satisfactory way of distributing the cost.

The networks are certain to argue, too, that the imposition of such a tax as I am proposing would put them out of business. They will argue this in the face of the annual reports which make an absurdity out of any such claim.

In an effort to divert attention in another direction, they will say, "If you are going to tax us in this manner, why not tax newspapers as well?" One hopes that it will be pointed out to them patiently, once more, that their existence is a *privilege* granted by the public, while the newspapers have been given a constitutional guarantee of their *right* to exist.

Another argument, one may be sure, is that the tax will work a great hardship on individual stations in the network. We will all be expected to be greatly touched by this solicitude on the part of the network managements for the stations which make their status, power, and profits possible, and to forget that this will be the first time they have ever exhibited such concern. The simple answer, again, is to look at the profit-and-loss statements. No matter how this relatively small amount of money is viewed, it cannot be inflated to anything more than 3.5 percent.

Not everyone outside the industry is going to be for public television, of course. Other arguments will be raised against it, in this most contentious of societies. But it would be difficult for any fair-minded person to argue against the right of public television to exist. And aside from the special interest groups, there are few people likely to deny the vision of what television might become for all of us when the Public Television Corporation begins to carry out the intents and purposes of the Act which created it. A glimpse of that better world on the tube has been given to us by E. B. White. In a letter to the Carnegie Commission, he wrote:

"Noncommercial television should address itself to the ideal of excellence, not the idea of acceptability—which is what keeps commercial television from climbing the staircase. I think television should be the visual counterpart of the literary essay, should arouse our dreams, satisfy our hunger for beauty, take us on journeys, enable us to participate in events, present great drama and music, explore the sea and the sky and the woods and the hills. It should be our Lyceum, our Chautauqua, our Minsky's, and our Camelot. It sould restate and clarify the social dilemma and the political pickle. Once in a while it does, and you get a quick glimpse of its potential."

# POSTSCRIPT

As I warned the reader at the beginning, this has been an angry letter, an ill-tempered book. By this time, however, I hope he will better understand what has inspired the anger and the ill temper. If I could sum it up in two words, I would say my anger—and now, I hope, yours—has been brought on by air pollution. We are poisoning our physical environment with smog and foul odors, and so are we poisoning our cultural environment with the triviality and worse of network television.

In this book I have set forth three objectives to counteract this pollution. First, I have advocated breaking up the massive triopoly which the networks represent. Second, I have urged that, regardless of whatever lip service may be paid to public television by the networks, they must not be permitted to stand in the way of realizing this much needed reform which the Public Television Act has made possible. Finally,

I have reminded the reader, in every way I know how, that it is his responsibility, if he wants better television, to exercise his right as a citizen in guaranteeing that the Federal Communications Commission does the work of regulation it was created to do. If the Commission is not constituted to perform its functions in these areas competently, then perhaps steps should be taken to reconstitute the Commission.

On our ability to bring these things about may well depend the political and cultural viability of this nation.

What do you think of *Open Letter From a Television Viewer?* Of the opinions expressed in it? Of Robert Montgomery's point of view?

Do you find Mr. Montgomery's arguments well-founded or fallacious? Do you feel that *Open Letter From a Television Viewer* takes its proper place in the Open Letter series whose purpose is to "discuss, dissect and delve into contemporary ideas and mores?"

Give us your opinions on *Open Letter From a Television Viewer.* We will be more than happy to discuss them with you, and we will invite Robert Montgomery to write to you, too.

JAMES H. HEINEMAN, INC.
60 East 42nd Street
New York, N. Y. 10017